"May the traditions of the
holidays bring you comfort and joy."

♡ Debbie Mumm

DEBBIE MUMM® JOYFUL TRADITIONS for the Holidays

Copyright 2001 by Landauer Corporation

Art Copyright 2001 by Debbie Mumm

This book was designed, produced, and published by Landauer Books
A division of Landauer Corporation
12251 Maffitt Road, Cumming, Iowa 50061

President: Jeramy Lanigan Landauer
Executive Vice President: Becky Johnston
Executive Vice President: James L. Knapp
Managing Editor: Marlene Hemberger Heuertz
Art Director: Laurel Albright
Creative Assistant: Kimberly O'Brien
Creative Contributor: Margaret Sindelar
Graphics Technician: Stewart Cott
Photographer: Craig Anderson Photography

ISBN: 1-890621-27-7
This book is printed on acid-free paper.

DEBBIE MUMM®

JOYFUL TRADITIONS
for
the Holidays

Table of Contents

Introduction

Christmas always seems to bring with it a flurry of activity centered around the traditional sights, scents, and sounds of the season. No matter how busy I may be, I find myself getting caught up in the magic and mystery of it all.

Many of my holiday designs, from jolly woodland Santas to smiling snowmen and shimmering snowflakes, are a reflection of my love for this merriest season of all.

The holidays are that special time of year when we take the time to express our love and share our hearts with others through handwritten notes on cards, thoughtful gifts, and festive gatherings of friends and families. Taking time to celebrate familiar customs and share in family traditions makes memories that will stay in our hearts forever. Building on joyful traditions from our past, holiday celebrations offer a wonderful opportunity to create new traditions for the next generation to carry into the future.

As you look forward to the holidays, keep in mind the simple joys of the season that will always be meant for sharing—faith, hope, love, and most of all, peace!

Debbie Mumm

Joyful Traditions...and how they came to be

Bringing nature home

The joyful traditions we celebrate during the holidays reach back hundreds of years to simpler times when the hearth was the heart of the home. The fire that offered warmth and light was also used for cooking and the fireplace became a natural gathering place for family and friends, especially as summer gave way to autumn and the days grew shorter and colder. The shortest day of the year, December 21, which marked the beginning of longer, light-filled days ahead, came to be known as the Winter Solstice. During the darkest days of the year as the eagerly-awaited Winter Solstice and the return of the sun approached, celebrations evolved to shake off the winter gloom. The Gothic name for the month of December, *juleiss*, means the month of celebrations and partying. The word "Yule" still exists in Dutch as *joel* or *jol*, translated as "loud, fun, rambunctious partying."

The custom of dragging a tree or a large log into the village or a home to be burned throughout the season of celebrating has come to be known as bringing in the Yule log. Special meaning was attached to ancient trees and evergreens, such as ivy, holly, and mistletoe, which all brought forth fruit in the winter. According to legend, Santa Claus lived in the forest and emerged wearing a green, fur-trimmed robe and carrying a horn, evergreens, or a small tree, and sometimes a fiery torch—all symbols of life and warmth, even in winter. Thus began the custom of bringing nature home with celebrations centered around the hearth as the heart of the home.

Heralding the season

From the biblical account of the angel who visited Mary bringing glad tidings of joy, to angelic hosts featured in paintings by the Great Masters, these heavenly beings have been traditionally portrayed as tall, winged, ethereal figures in flowing robes.

However, the Florentine sculptor Donatello changed all that with his famous *Cantorium* showing dozens of dancing cherubs, celebrating the joys of divine music. After Donatello, it became the norm for angels to be depicted as innocent, fun-loving, miniature people. These rosy-cheeked creatures assumed a powerful role as privileged intercessors between the worldly and the spiritual realms. Cherubs were featured prominently in the paintings of Raphael, Titian, and Rubens, and then went into a decline with the waning of the Rococo style.

But during the Victorian era they experienced a revival with the emphasis on nostalgia and sentiment. Cherubs were reproduced on greeting cards and valentines, and as elaborate cut-outs and embossed figures. Cherubs declined again during the Modernist movement, but have experienced new popularity as messengers of sentiment and spirituality. Angels, in the form of fun-loving cherubs, are the perfect images for heralding the season.

Decking the halls

Much of the preparation for the feasts that followed the final harvest in November and continued on through the month of December centered around filling homes or banquet halls with symbols of the season—evergreens, wreaths, and the ivy, holly, and mistletoe that bore fruit in the winter. The oak tree was considered sacred, so it became customary to cut down a lowly pine tree to bring inside and dress up with garlands, candles, and other decorations.

With the festively decorated walls and tree, a Yule log burning brightly in the fireplace, tables loaded with a tantalizing feast, and carefully wrapped gifts waiting to be opened, even the smallest of homes became an inviting haven for celebration. Through the years, decking the halls has become synonymous with creating a holiday home overflowing with welcome and warmth.

Sharing good cheer

The feasts and celebrations welcoming the Winter Solstice originated as a means to mark the past harvest and the beginning of longer, sunlit days and the new growth anticipated in the Spring.

As these festive gatherings continued through the centuries, the birth of Christ also came to be celebrated at the end of December. With it came the gift of the Magi and the tradition of sharing gifts "from the heart" with friends and family. The customs of bringing nature home, heralding the season, and decking the halls all have one purpose in common—sharing good cheer with friends and family!

©Debbie Mumm

Bringing Nature Home

© Debbie Mumm

Bringing Nature Home

Gather the last leaves of autumn and the bounty of the harvest to get an early start on holiday decorating by bringing nature home. On the following pages, you'll find a forest of inviting ideas for transitioning your home from harvest to holiday in no time at all.

Begin with a palette of butternut and goldenrod accented with maple leaf red and branch out to deeper shades of gold and cranberry later in the season. Mix the contrasting textures of sugar pinecones and pineapples with kumquats and acorn squash. Combine clusters of nuts and berries with roadside naturals such as grapevines, dried milkweed pods, and ornamental grasses. Later, add winter blooming evergreens— holly, ivy, and mistletoe to create branch-built bouquets.

Layer it all together in garlands, wreaths, baskets, and bowls for a natural finish for your holiday decorating.

©Debbie Mumm

$\mathcal{L}$ooking much like the trees they become, a festive trio of gold painted pinecones each in a painted terra cotta saucer, brightly illuminates a holiday tabletop setting.

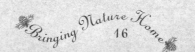

$\mathcal{E}$arly celebrations of the Winter Solstice (the shortest day of the year bringing with it the promise of Spring) often began in early November, following the final harvest. It was natural to fill the house with garlands of greens embellished with gourds, pinecones, and autumn leaves brightly burnished by the late summer sun. For more natural flair, place a large vase inside a leaf-covered grapevine wreath. Transform the vase into a luminaria with a candle surrounded by nuts and pinecones.

Woodchopper Santa

© Debbie Mumm

Santa, the legendary woodsman, is right at home with a stack of logs. Bring nature home to your guests with a tiny pinecone in a painted terra cotta pot. Accent it with a crackle finish and a handwritten name for a party favor to personalize each guest's place setting.

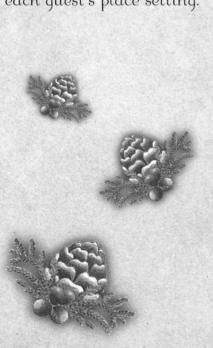

Crystal reflects the mood and magic of Christmas—when even the ordinary becomes bright and shiny with holiday splendor. It's easy to fill your favorite crystal bowl with glass ornaments, center it in a wreath of variegated holly, and add accents of elegant red roses and ribbon.

Bringing nature home is as simple as surprising your guests with a healthy holiday treat—ordinary trail mix served in a crystal candy dish!

$\mathcal{W}$elcome guests and family alike with the traditional symbol of hospitality—
a fresh pineapple nestled in a wreath along with kumquats, leaves, and red berries.

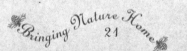

Traditionally, in Colonial America, fresh fruit was considered a rare and welcome treat for the holidays. Children eagerly looked forward to finding an orange in the toe of their Christmas stockings. For a similar treat, you can fill an old-fashioned market basket with greens and fresh fruits for a taste of holiday enjoyment.

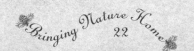

Woodland Santa

Christmas Eve Chapel

WELCOME

CHRISTMAS EVE
SERVICE

Parson
Brown

©Debbie Mumm

Celebrating Christmas Eve in a candlelit church service is a meaningful tradition for many families. Create a simple centerpiece for a tabletop with a favorite holiday-themed framed picture surrounded by greens and roses in gold baskets. Or, bring home an armful of fresh flowers (in water tubes from the florist), and wrap with bright tissue and ribbon for almost instant decorating!

$\mathcal{J}$ ust as the ring, an unending circle, has long been a symbol of eternity, wreaths have become a symbol of nature's eternal bounty. Lavish a grapevine wreath with dried florals and dozens of favorite miniatures to celebrate the holidays naturally.

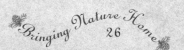

Bountiful Birdhouses

©Debbie Mumm

$\mathcal{F}$rom country to contemporary, birdhouses are inviting decorating accents and reminders that the holidays are a natural time for sharing food and friendship—especially with a few of our fine feathered friends. Inexpensive, unpainted birdhouses go contemporary with white paint and Snowtex® on roofs.

Decorate now and feed the birds later with a tabletop collection that's "for the birds!"

Fun for now and food for later, fill half-rounds of scooped out oranges with birdseed—natural ingredients that can go outside, to carry on the tradition of giving even after the holidays are over.

©Debbie Mumm

Heralding
the Season

©Debbie Mumm

Heralding the Season

Greeting the season can be as simple as sending out holiday cards with handwritten notes or as elaborate as an open house for a hundred or more guests. Whether your approach to celebrating the holiday season is spontaneous or planned to perfection, it's often the small things that set the mood for this magical season of joy and reunion.

Traditions steeped in time and memory often set the scene for the days ahead. Finding the perfect tree, carefully unwrapping ornaments that have been handed down from mother to daughter, baking cookies, wrapping gifts, lighting candles—all keep the spirit of Christmas alive in hearts and homes. On the following pages, discover easy and inexpensive inspirations for heralding the season in holiday style!

Gloria

Melody

Angelica

Regina

Goodwill to All

©Debbie Mumm

Truly the light is sweet,
and a pleasant thing it is
for the eyes to behold

©Debbie Mumm

$\mathcal{D}$eck the halls and scent the walls with holiday sachets smelling of gingerbread, pine, o
bayberry. Display sachets on a fabric or paper-lined frame, minus the glass.

*E*levate plain vanilla candles to new heights of holiday splendor. Fill glass cylinders with pinecones and miniature wooden apples, and top it all off with the warm glow of candlelight.

Holly Angel

©Debbie Mumm

$\mathcal{S}$et the scene for angel's wings and other things by wrapping the bannister in white twinkle lights covered with a cloud of white tulle, shimmering snowflakes, sheer ribbon, and translucent paper wings cut from vellum.

𝒲ho needs a tree for displaying a favorite collection of gold and silver ornaments?
Show them off on a stack of glass cake stands in a sparkling silver-frosted setting—
complete with angel food cake!

$\mathcal{B}$bring out your treasured keepsakes—from quotes to candlesticks—and share them with the world. Setting a framed mirror on a tabletop creates an illusion of more than meets the eye.

Angels capture love and sprinkle it upon our hearts.

DEBBIE MUMM®

©Debbie Mumm

$\mathcal{L}$ight the way to special holiday gatherings with votives in punched tin "pails" on the porch, patio, or a picket fence. Snippets of evergreens and gold mesh are weatherproof.

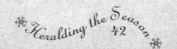

Star Sprinkler

©Debbie Mumm

*M*ake music for the holidays with bells, traditional symbols of the season, displayed in non-traditional settings. Add bells, bows, and snowmen to painted wooden embroidery hoops, or cover heart-shaped foam with a myriad of gold and silver jingle bells in assorted sizes.

Snowflake Delivery

©Debbie Mumm

$\mathcal{S}$end sentiments of the season to someone special. Fill a mug with a package of hot cocoa mix and mini marshmallows, make matching coasters, and wrap it all up in gold mesh fabric tied with ribbon. Coasters are snowmen cut from stationery and decoupaged on glass backed with felt and trimmed with copper foil cut with edging scissors.

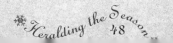

andcrafted gift tags can be scrap-crafting sensations with a little imagination. Cut small squares of felt with edgers and glue textured paper to either side. On the front, add a solo snowman button and use the back for writing names as shown here.

Elderberry's Gifts

©Debbie Mumm

$\mathcal{W}$hat could be more heavenly than an angel choir? Simply make a color copy of any of the angels from the following pages, glue to foam core, and cut out the shape carefully with a sharp art knife.

*F*or easy window or door decor, enlarge all four angels to fit your space and arrange them accordingly. Here, an antique door gets dressed up for the holidays by dividing the frosted glass into quadrants with ribbon before adding the heavenly host.

©Debbie Mumm

©Debbie Mumm

Heralding the Season
53

©Debbie Mumm

Goodwill to All

©Debbie Mumm

Decking the Halls

Decking the halls may be the most fun you've had in a long time when you think "quick and easy."

Transform ordinary rooms into holiday sensations with just a few decorative accessories and accents. Focus on simple garlands, wreaths, centerpieces, and new ways to display collections and keepsakes you already have on hand. Using more imagination than money, you'll soon see why decking the halls continues to be a timeless holiday tradition!

©Debbie Mumm

©Debbie Mumm

$\mathcal{D}$uring the Victorian era, a stolen kiss under the mistletoe meant marriage in the near future. To honor this quaint custom, elaborate kissing balls graced the halls of many a fine home. It's easy to create your own kissing ball by covering a foam ball with round, red push pins and holly leaves with a ribbon-tied sprig of mistletoe.

$\mathcal{G}$arlands formerly graced with autumn's harvest gather holiday spirit with a sprinkling of gold, white, and touches of true Christmas red in the kissing ball, quilts, wreaths, poinsettias, and elegant ribbon accents scattered throughout the holiday home.

Small space holiday decorating calls for creative solutions. In place of a towering pine, substitute tiny soft-sculpture trees or feathery Norfolk pines planted in painted pots.

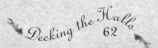

Decked Out Igloo

©Debbie Mumm

Two Friends in a Stocking

©Debbie Mumm

Delight a collector with the decorative accents on stamps. Start a custom of saving holiday stamps from year to year for creative displays or cut them from printed fabric as shown here.

$\mathcal{F}$or a fun conversation piece, pair up a serious Victorian sleigh with your favorite goofy-guy craft creation and watch for smiles from young and old alike.

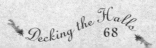

Bringing Home Christmas

©Debbie Mumm

Village Tree Lighting

©Debbie Mumm

*L*ight up the night with ethereal grapevine globes that are stunning in their simplicity. For each, insert a string of twinkle lights into a gold painted grapevine ball and place it on a clear glass candlestick for a floating sensation.

$\mathcal{W}$hat could be quicker than quick? For decorating that takes under a minute, tie scraps of ribbon into bows to top off a trio of brass candlesticks nestled in greens.

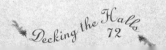

$\mathcal{T}$reat your guests to a swag of color overhead by combining variegated holly with festive printed ribbon. Or, for a cost-effective centerpiece, combine a few red roses with inexpensive alstroemeria.

Winter Gardener

©Debbie Mumm

$\mathscr{D}$iscover how easy it is for traditional glass ball ornaments handed down from past generations to share the space with everything from a watering can to woodland Santa ornament.

$\mathcal{F}$or a little variety, transform a perfectly plain coatrack into charming holiday decor by putting the shelf to work holding collections instead of caps and using the hooks for hanging wreaths. Here, snowmen ceramics include collector plates, cookie jars, and a musical snow globe.

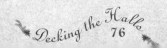

Igloo Village Carolers

©Debbie Mumm

Sharing
Good Cheer

Sharing Good Cheer

All the magic and mystery of Christmas comes together in the beloved customs and family traditions that spring forth from embracing a spirit of generosity. Reaching out to friends and family with gifts, greetings, and small tokens of appreciation at this time of the year seems as natural as breathing. We do it so spontaneously that it seems like it must be in the air along with the snowflakes that drift down so effortlessly. On the following pages discover tempting treats for kids and easy inspirations for sharing good cheer with everyone on your gift list!

©Debbie Mumm

$\mathcal{M}$ix up a big batch of sugar cookie dough and turn the kids loose with cookie cutters and frosting tubes. For a special place setting, fill a custard cup with sugar and let each child's creative snowman cookie skate on thin ice—complete with a posted sign!

©Debbie Mumm

*R*eminiscent of antique feather trees, this sturdy white wire variation provides the perfect parking place for star-shaped ornaments and cookies in cellophane bags.

Sugar Cookies

2 1/2 cups all-purpose flour
1 cup sugar
1 cup butter, softened
1 egg
1 teaspoon baking powder
2 tablespoons orange juice
1 tablespoon vanilla

Directions:

In large mixing bowl, combine all ingredients. Beat at low speed, scraping bowl often, until well mixed. Cover. Refrigerate at least 2 hours.

Heat oven to 400 degrees. On lightly floured surface, roll out dough, one-third at a time to 1/4-inch thickness. Cut with cookie cutters and place 1 inch apart on cookie sheets.

Bake for 6 to 10 minutes or until edges are lightly browned. Cool completely before frosting.

Makes 36 cookies.

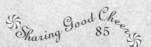

F or a welcome surprise, stack up colorful treats such as popcorn balls, decorated sugar cookies, and tiny packages on a three-tiered stand usually reserved for plates. Serve with peppermint tea or holiday punch.

Popcorn Balls

1 cup unpopped corn

Syrup:
1 cup sugar
1 cup white corn syrup
1 package of any flavor
of Jell-O®

Directions:
Pop corn according to package
directions. Combine sugar, corn
syrup, and Jell-O® in a stovetop
pan. Boil until dissolved and
pour over popped corn. Let cool a
little before making into balls.

Makes 10-12 three-inch balls.

Creating a custom that kids can count on year after year and never outgrow is a challenge. Begin by personalizing a special ornament with a nametag for sharing good cheer on Christmas morning. After breakfast, add it to the collection on the tree that will continue to grow year after year.

The secret to snowy white frosting covered in drifts of coconut flakes? Meringue that covers the cake and is popped into the oven at 300 degrees— just long enough to set the meringue and brown the tips of the peaks. Top it all off with a dusting of crushed candy mints!

$\mathcal{M}$ake a meal special for kids, too, with party-favor mugs to take home.
Fill a mug with candy canes or a chocolate cupcake topped with crushed peppermint.

Sweet Gingerland

©Debbie Mumm

Holiday Teapots

©Debbie Mumm

$\mathcal{E}$ven the kitchen deserves a wreath of its own. Every year add another teapot and watch your collection grow—perhaps with a little help from your friends and family!

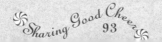

$\mathcal{S}$heets of stickers or stickers for the wall, appropriately named Wallies®, offer lots of ways to dress up plain glass containers—from Mason to jelly jars. Fill the clean, empty jars with homemade treats, candy, cocoa mix, or even a candle. Personalize plain blank journals by adding stickers, fabric, buttons, or a bookmark.

𝒯urn lunchtime into funtime with a tiny lunchbox lined with holiday tissue and filled with star-shaped peanut butter and jelly sandwiches (cut with a cookie cutter), chips, baby carrots for dipping, and for dessert—mini pretzels already dipped in chocolate!

*N*ot just any lunchbox, this one of a kind wonder is filled with fun expressions of good cheer—complete with a perky angel pal holding a personalized place card.

Gifted Snowman

©Debbie Mumm

$\mathcal{T}$erra cotta pots can hold much more than plants when you wrap them in festive fabric and bows. Fill a pot with kitchen treats and towels for the office exchange or a last-minute gift that is already wrapped and ready to go! For more quick gifts, keep a friendship basket near the front door and fill it with small surprises wrapped in over-sized boxes.

Polar Express

©Debbie Mumm

𝒫illows take on an unexpected holiday flair when paired with lavish ribbon bows.

$\mathscr{E}$xpress sentiments of the season you wish to share with others on engraved stones spray painted gold. Fill a satin box with the golden messages, and top off the lid with a keepsake snowflake ornament.

Snowflake Lady

©Debbie Mumm

Sources

©Debbie Mumm

For over a decade Debbie Mumm's charming images and distinctive style have captured the hearts and imaginations of millions.

The CEO and Creative Director of the company that bears her name, Debbie Mumm is a prolific artist and designer who finds a steady stream of inspiration from her surroundings and even everyday activities. Part of her gift is interpreting her observations in a fresh, new, original way.

Debbie loves the thrill of creating new artwork and she is dedicated to seeing it translated into beautiful, high quality, loveable products. She communicates a genuine warmth and kindness through her designs which is the reason people respond so positively to her work.

The author of more than forty books on quilting and home decorating, Debbie began her business as a quilt and fabric designer. Today, more than forty companies have licensing agreements with Debbie Mumm, Inc. and her designs can be seen on products ranging from dinnerware to greeting cards.

Decorating is a personal passion for Debbie and something that she does for her own enjoyment. She finds decorating to be an outlet for self-expression, creativity, and innovation. She loves to use everyday items in new ways to create totally different seasonal looks for her home.

Debbie's passions for decorating and holiday celebrations were the inspirations for *Debbie Mumm® Joyful Traditions for the Holidays*. Debbie believes that home decorating is an opportunity to discover your own creativity and a meaningful outlet for self-expression.

Part of her gift is to find the
visual richness in everything that she sees
and to interpret it in a fresh, original way.

Santa's Village Elves' Bunkhouse

ELVES' BUNK HOUSE

©Debbie Mumm

Beautiful Artwork and
High-Quality Products

Debbie Mumm's delightfully detailed artwork can be found on hundreds of high-quality products.

Dinnerware sets for both holiday enjoyment and everyday use feature Debbie's beautiful borders, fresh color palettes, and whimsical characters. Many of these designs are enhanced by hand-painted accessories including cookie jars, serving trays, mini teapots, salt and pepper shakers, and creamer/sugar sets.

Debbie has also created a memorable line of greeting cards featuring timeless artwork and sweet sentiments. You can find these and a host of other stationery products including calendars, journals, notepads, and note cards at gift and specialty stores.

If you have a passion for scrapbooking, look for a full line of charming Debbie Mumm® papers, stickers, frames, and albums in a variety of sizes and styles. Whether you are looking for novelty papers or something a bit more classic, you'll find them in the Debbie Mumm® scrapbooking collection.

A house becomes a warm and comfortable home with wallpapers and borders designed by Debbie Mumm®. Creating a beautifully decorated home is effortless with coordinated lamps, occasional pieces, and wall art featuring Debbie's charming watercolor designs.

To find out more about Debbie Mumm® products, please visit our website at www.debbiemumm.com. Hundreds of Debbie Mumm® products are offered online for easy purchase. You'll also find feature articles on home decorating, gardening, cooking, and holidays. New quilting and craft projects are featured monthly, including tips and techniques. Visit the online world of Debbie Mumm® today.